The Sounds of Sicilian

An Interactive Pronunciation Guide

Gaetano Cipolla
The Sounds of Sicilian: An Interactive Pronunciation Guide
ISBN 978-1-881901-51-8

Acknowledgements

We are grateful for the generous grant from the International Center for Writing and Translation at the University of California, Irvine, that in part made the publication of this work possible. Many thanks also to Prof. Frank Cannonito and to Dr. J. Kirk Bonner for theIr help and suggestions as well as to Prof. Salvatore Riolo. Finally, I thank Florence Russo-Cipolla for her invaluable help in recording the CD. I also thank Jerry, Brian and Greg of the Radio Station at St. John's Unwersity for the use of their recording facilities and technical assistance. Finally, many thanks to Art Dieli for remastering and polishing the recording.

For Information and orders write to:

Legas

Po. Box 149
Mineola, New York
11501 USA

3 Wood Aster Bay
Ottawa, Ontario
K2R 1D3 Canada

Legaspublishing.com

Printed in March 2015 by Gauvin Press, Gatineau, Québec

Gaetano Cipolla

The Sounds of Sicilian

An Interactive Pronunciation Guide

LEGAS

Table of Contents

Introduction

The pronunciation of Sicilian should not present insurmountable difficulties for anyone. It will be especially easy for those who are familiar with romance languages like Italian, Spanish, French, Portuguese and Rumanian. Sicilian was the first of the regional languages of Italy to gain acceptance as a medium for poetic expression. It flourished under the reign of Frederick II in the first half of the thirteenth century. The poets who belonged to the Sicilian School, some of whom were not native of Sicily, wrote in the language spoken at the imperial court. Sicilian was the language used to record the actions of the Sicilian Parliament until the middle of the sixteenth century when Florentine replaced it in official documents. Until the first half of the twentieth century, Sicilian continued to be the only language of most inhabitants of the island. Italian was learned in school and even though official business was conducted in Italian, the majority of Sicilians used their language in their daily lives and they still do so today. Although linguists announced its imminent disappearance 50 years ago, Sicilian has proven to be resilient. Though its range has been restricted to use within the family, among friends and relatives, Sicilian is still spoken and understood by most people on the island. Although Sicilian political institutions have not done enough to preserve it, interest in it as the language of poetry and the performing arts has been growing. Many people in Sicily and in the United States are interested in seeing the language preserved. In the United States, Arba Sicula has devoted all its energies to the study, preservation and dissemination of Sicilian for the past 25 years. The present undertaking, long in coming, answers a need often expressed by our members and by those who want to make a connection with the language of their ancestors. Used in combination with our bilingual journal and with our other publications on Sicilian grammar, this guide to the pronunciation of Sicilian will be a very useful and welcome tool of study.

The sounds of Sicilian are basically similar to those of the other romance languages and, needless to say, they are closest to Italian, even though Sicilian has a few sounds that are not present in Italian, such as the retroflex sound that linguists transcribe with "dd" and sometimes with dots under the "dd" as in *beddu* (beautiful), and the sound of *ciu* in *ciuri* that linguists have represented in various ways for centuries without ever reaching agreement. Though not unique to Sicilian, these two sounds represent one of the distinguishing features of the language. If you are not a native Sicilian, people say, you will have difficulty producing them, especially the "dd" sound. We are confident, however, that with practice you will be able to master them. We will see how these sounds can be produced later.

The Sicilian Alphabet

There are 23 letters in the Sicilian alphabet. The letters "k," "y", "x" and "w" are not used except in words of foreign origin. There have been some attempts to revive some of these letters to return to the spelling Sicilians used centuries ago, but today those who write in Sicilian often do not abide by generally accepted rules of spelling. This has resulted in a less than uniform system of writing. The 23 letters of the Sicilian alphabet are:

Letter	Name of Letter	English Pronunciation
A	a	ah
B	bi	bee
C	ci	tchee
D	di	dee
Dd	ddi	ddhee
E	e	eh
F	effi	ehffee
G	gi	jee
H	acca	ahkha
I	i	ee
J	i longa	eeh longah
L	elli	ehllie
M	emmi	ehmmie
N	enni	ehnnie
O	o	oh
P	pi	ppee
Q	cu	ckoo

R	erri	ehrrie
S	essi	ehssie
T	ti	ttee
U	u	ooh
V	vi or vu	vvee, vvooh
Z	zeta	dzetah

The Sicilian Vowel System

Let us begin with the vowel sounds. Unlike Italian, Sicilian has only five vowel sounds and they are:

a e i o u

Italian recognizes 7 vowel sounds because the "e" and the "o" can be pronounced as an open or closed sound. Sicilian pronounces the "e" and the "o" as open sounds as in such English words "bet" "let" and "not" "more". Sicilian vowels, unlike English vowels, are always pronounced in one way, no matter where they occur.

Thus the "a" of "casa," and "pani," is like the "a" in "father";
the "e" of "genti," "meti" is like the "e" of "let";
the "o" of "mori," "robba" is like the "o" of "over";
the "i" of "Pippinu," "minnali," is like the "i" of "machine";
the "u" of "subbitu," "omu" is like the "oo" of "stoop"

Sometimes, however, Sicilian vowels, because they are in unstressed positions, tend to be pronounced as a blend of two vowels. This occurs usually in the third person plural of the present or imperfect tenses and in some words. For example, the present and imperfect tenses of verbs like *purtari* (to bring) can be heard as *portanu*, or *portunu; purtavanu* or *purtavunu;* words like *subbitu* (right away) can be heard as *subbutu.* These vowels are called uncertain because the speaker does not stress the vowel in question and its pronunciation can be heard as either "a" or "u".

The Sounds of Sicilian Consonants

Sicilian consonants for the most part are pronounced almost exactly as the Italian counterparts. There are, however, a few excep-

9

tions, as we will see. English speakers will not find it very difficult to pronounce Sicilian sounds.

B

B has the same sound as the "b" in "bed". This letter presents a peculiarity that is true of other Sicilian letters such as the **"d,"** **"r"**, and the **"z"**. In initial and also in medial position, the "b" is pronounced double. Words normally written with one "b" are pronounced double as in the following: *bonu, beddu, bastuni* and *babbu* (good, beautiful, stick and dumb). Even if the "b" occurs in the middle of the word the sound is pronounced as though it were a double consonant. This does not mean you pronounce the letter twice, it simply means that the vowel that precedes the double sound is shorter than normal. This will take some practice because English does not make much use of the double consonant sound. It does occur in compound words such as "bookkeeping" or "good day". The sound is made primarily by pausing slightly after the vowel that precedes the double consonant. Try pausing in pronouncing the following words: *à bbitu, sà bbatu, sù bbitu.* Now pronounce the words at nomal speed: *àbbitu, sàbbatu* and *sùbbitu* (suit, Saturday and right away). The pause will help you to pronounce double consonants which occur frequently and affect most sounds, except the *sci, gli,* and *gn* sounds. Practice with the following pairs: *Caru/carru; Vini/vinni; Nanna/nana; Spisa/spissu; Jattu/Jatu; Cottu/cotu; Ccani/cani; Assai/usai; Potti/poti; Viti/vitti.*

C

C has either a hard sound (k) as in *cani* (dog) or a soft sound (ch) as in *celu* (sky). If the "c" is followed by the vowels *"a," "o," "u"* or the letter *"h"*, it has a hard sound as in the English consonant k. If the "c" is followed by the vowels "e" and "i", then the sound is pronounced as the English words *check* and *chin*. Thus, if we add the five vowel sounds of Sicilian *a, e, i, o, u,* to the "c" we will get the following sounds *ca, che, chi, co, cu.* Note how in order to obtain the had sounds of *che* and *chi* we placed an "h" between the "c" and the two vowels. If the h were absent, the two sounds would be pronounced with a soft "c": *ce* and *ci*. Pronounce the following words:

cani, chesa, china, cori, cuda (dog, church, full, heart, tail). The "h",
of course, was used to write the words *chesa* and *china*. The English
"ch" is made by placing an *e* or *i* after the "c". If other vowels follow
the *e* or *i* sometimes you will pronounce both of them as one sound,
as in *cia, ciu*, or as separate vowels as in *ceusa*. Repeat the following
words: *cessu, cinima, Ciullu, ciaula* (toilet, movie, Ciullu, crow).

The "c" in initial position is usually single, while in medial
position it is usually double: for example: *chiavi, chiovu*, but *occhiu,
specchiu* (key, nail, and eye, mirror). A peculiarity of the *parrata*, that
is, the subdialect of Ragusa in the southeastern part of Sicily is that
these same words are pronounced with a soft "c" as *chavee, chovoo,
occhoo, spehcchoo.*

The letter "c" has also been used to reproduce a special sound of
certain Sicilian words that are derived from Latin, words beginning
with *fl*, such as *flumen* (river) or *florem* (flower), which in Sicilian
became *ciumi* and *ciuri*. Specialists on the Sicilian language have
been arguing for centuries on how to write this sound. Today you
may see it written as *ciu* or *sciu*. Without going into the technical
explanation of how the sound is made, you can come very close to
it if you say "shoe" keeping your tongue well inside your mouth,
instead of holding it between the teeth. A puff of air should come
out of your mouth in pronouncing *ciumi, ciuri*. If the stress falls on
the succeeding syllable, however, as in *ciusciàri*, the initial sound is
made further back in the mouth and no air should escape. Repeat
the following words: *ciocca, ciauru, ciariari, ciumara* (hen, smell, to
smell, riverbed).

<h2 style="text-align:center">D</h2>

D is slightly different from the English "d". The d of "dog" or
"dig" is more explosive than the Sicilian "d" of *dumani* or *dopu* where
the "d" is pronounced with the tongue completely inside the mouth
rather than between the teeth. This letter, depending on where you
are in Sicily will be pronounced as an "r", as in the words *duminica/
ruminica, dota/rota, nidu/niru, dici/rici* (Sunday, dowery, nest, says),
and as a "t" in and around Messina in initial and in unstressed positions, as in *denti/tenti, diavulu/tiavulu* and *tebbidu/tebbitu*, (tooth,

devil, tepid). When the "d" is followed by a vowel in unstressed position such as in *vidu, cridu* (I see, I believe), it changes to a "y" sound. In Sicilian the "y" sound is written with a "j". Thus *vidu, cridu* change to *viju, criju*.

Unlike Italian, the "d" can be pronounced as a double consonant even in initial positions, as in *ddimoniu, ddibbulizza, ddebbitu* (demon, weakness, debt), as well as in medial position as in *addumannari, addurmirisi, addunarisi* (to ask, to fall asleep, to notice). This double "dd" sound is not to be confused with the retroflex sound of *beddu, Turiddu* (beautiful and Turiddu) that we will describe shortly. In the first examples, *addumannari*, the double "dd" is made by shortening the preceding vowel and striking the bottom of your upper teeth with the tip of your tongue protruding slightly beyond them. Remember to pause after the initial vowel. In the following examples the double "dd" is pronounced as above: *addinucchiari, addisiari, addivintari, arridduciri* (to kneel, to yearn for, to become, to reduce). This is the same as the Italian sound *addormentarsi* (to fall asleep).

The d and the t followed by an r have a distinctive Sicilian sound, different from Italian. Such words as *ddrittu, draddraia* (straight, witch) and *trenu, tronu* (train, thunder) are pronounced with the tongue inside your mouth rather than between the teeth, as in the English "dry" and "train". The double dd of *Turiddu* is described in the next section.

Dd

Dd. The "dd" sound is made almost exactly as in such American English words as "caddy," daddy" "batty". Pronounce the following words and observe how the tongue curls a bit and then strikes the upper part of the palate: *beddu,* (beautiful) *liveddu* (level), *cuteddu* (knife), *purceddu* (pig), *agneddu* (lamb), *capiddi* (hair), **munzedda** (mounds), *Mungibbeddu* (Mt. Etna), *jaddina* (chicken), *jaddu* (rooster), *madduni* (brick, tile), *cavaddu* (horse), *nuddu* (no one). In certain parts of Sicily, primarily in the western part, the "dd" sound above is made by adding a slight trill to it, so that when the sounds are written they add an "r". In Trapani, for example, the words above will be pronounced *beddru, liveddru, cuteddru, purceddru, agneddru, capiddri, munzeddra, Mungibbeddru, jaddrina*, etc...

F

F. The "f" sound presents no difficulty whatsover. It is the same as the English f as in *fame, film*. Pronounce the following: *fami* (hunger), *filu* (thread), *feli* (bile), *fulinia* (cobweb), *fogghia* (leaf), *chiffari* (things to do), *affettu* (affection), *fuddittu* (sprite).

G

G. The "g" sound presents the same difficulties as the "c". G has either a hard sound (go) as in *gamma* or a soft sound (jet) as in *genti*. If the "g" is followed by the vowels *a, o, u,* or the letter *h,* it has a hard sound as in "go". Repeat the following: *gattu, gamma, gaddu, gaggia, ghiommaru* (cat, leg, rooster, cage, ball of thread). If the "g" is followed by the vowels *e* and *i,* then the sound is pronounced as the English "j" as in the following words: *raggiuni, giovani, gilusia, gebbia* (reason, young person, jealousy, water tank). In some *parrati* of central Sicily the initial hard "g" drops off and the five words above will be pronounced as *àttu, àmma, àddu, àggia, òmmaru*. The same words, however, will be pronounced as *jattu, jàmma, jaddu, jommaru* in eastern Sicily (Messina, Catania). The combination "g" plus "r" in such words as *granni, grossu, grutta* (big, large, cave) in many parts of Sicily will also lose the "g" and will be pronounced *ranni, rossu, rutta*.

The "gn" combination is similar to its Italian counterpart and to the Spanish "ñ" sound. It is equivalent to the sound of *canyon* or *onion*. Pronounce the following words: *castagna, vegnu, tigna, vigna, signali* (chestnut, I am coming, bald head, vineyard, signal). Differentiate between this sound and words like *Catania, ddimoniu, tistimoniu* (Catania, demon, witness).

Another sound peculiar to Romance languages that is written with a "gli" in Italian and with a "ll" in Spanish exists in Sicilian in certain areas, but for the majority of speakers on the island this sound has been replaced by "gghi". Thus, where Italian will have *famiglia, figlio, foglio, taglio, travagliare*, (Family, son, sheet of paper, cut, travail-work) Sicilian will have *famigghia, figghiu, fogghiu, tag-ghiu, travagghiari.*

H

H has no sound of its own. Its only purpose is to make a soft *c* or *g* into a hard *c* or *g*. *Cetu* (social rank) becomes *chetu* (quiet) by placing an h after the c. *Gettu* becomes *ghettu* by placing the h after the g.

J

The "j" in Sicilian is equivalent to the English "y". It is a consonant that is slowly disappearing and being replaced by the Italian vowel i. In the past, words such as *boja, noja, gioja* (executioner, boredom, joy) used to be written with a j. Today they are being replaced by the Italian "i" as in *boia, noia, gioia*. Nevertheless the j has a role to play and its pronunciation requires some attention. It occurs in words such as *jornu, jiri, jurnata, Japicu, jitu, jenniru, jardinu, jaddu* (day, to go, length of day, Jacob, finger, son-in-law, garden, rooster) etc… If pronounced separately or if it is preceded by an unstressed word the j in these words is simply equivalent to the English y. Thus the j of *jorna* preceded by an unstressed word such as *cincu* or *quattru* will be pronounced *cincu jorna, quattru jorna.* (five days, four days) But if the words beginning with "j" are preceded by monosyllables such as *tri* and *a*, the combination will be pronounced *trigghiorna, agghiurnata* (Three days, for the day) even though *jornu* is still written with a "j" . Before titles such as *San*, and *Don* as in *Japicu, Jachinu* the resulting sound would be *dongnabicu, dongnachinu.* Following the word *ogni* (every) as in *ogni jornu*, the combination would be pronounced *ognigghiornu* and in the area of Messina and province *ogningnornu*. A sentence that is written as *"a jiri a vidiri a don Jachinu"* (I have to go see Don Jachinu) would sound like *"agghiri avvidiri a donGnachinu."* In some parrati the "v" in stressed position may be pronounced as a "b". Thus *avvidiri* could be pronounced as *abbidiri.*

L

The **L** presents no difficulty when it is in initial position. Thus the "l" of the following is the same as the English "love". *Lana, lena, linu, lona, luna, mulu, mali, meli.* The double "ll" exists in certain Gallo-Italic areas (Bronte, Maletto, Randazzo, S. Domenica) and in most of Sicily for words that have been borrowed from Italian such as *ballu, cristallu, ribbelli*, (dance, crystal, rebel), however, the double "ll" in most parts of Sicily became the retroflex sound "dd" we already discussed. Thus words that in Italian would be written as *collo, bellezza, cavallo, gallo* (neck, beauty, horse, rooster) in Sicilian became *coddu, biddizza, cavaddu* and *jaddu.*

The "l" followed by a **c**, an **m** or a **v** as in *falcu, calmu, salvu* (falcon, calm, safe) generally lose the "l" in favor of an "r", becoming *farcu, carmu, sarvu* in most parts of Sicily. The same words in the eastern part lose the "r" and double the consonant that follows as *faccu, cammu, savvu*, and in the area around Palermo, speakers will add a trailing "i" to the stressed syllable and pronounce the words *faiccu, caimmu, saivvu.*

M

The **M** does not present any difficulties for English speakers. It has the same sound as the "m" in *man, merit.* The "m" that follows a stressed vowel usually is pronounced double as in *càmmira, fìmmina, nùmmiru, cucùmmaru,* (room, woman, number, watermelon) etc... In Italian the combination *mb* is usually changed to *mm* in Sicilian as in the case of *gamba/jamma; piombo/chiummu; colomba/palumma* (leg, led, dove).

N

The **N** does not present any difficulties for English speakers. It is the same as the English "n" in *name.* Pronounce the following words: *Navi, ninna nanna, niuru, nudu, panuzzu* (Ship, lullaby, black, naked, bread). When the "n" is followed by a "d" in Italian, it generally changes to a double "n" in Sicilian, as in *rutunnu, munnu, funnu, quannu, munnizza* (round, world, bottom, when, garbage). The "d" sound is retained in a small area around Messina where such words would sound like *mundu, quandu, mundizza* etc...

The combination of *nv* of such words as *nvernu, nvidia, nvitu, cunventu* (winter, envy, invitation, convent) in most areas changes to *mmernu, mmidia, mmitu, cummentu* in the spoken language.

The combination **ng** merits special attention. Sicilian words such as *sangu, fangu, longu* (blood, mud, long) are not pronounced at all as their Italian counterparts *sangue, fango, lungo*. Nor are they pronounced as the English words "longer, finger". The Sicilian sound is closer to the *ng* of the English "Long Island" or "hanger" where the sound is made by withdrawing the tongue towards the back of the mouth. Pronounce these words: *rangu, sgangu, ngagghiari, ngratu, nfangatu* (rank, bunch, to catch, ingrate, muddy).

P

The **P** is similar to the English "p," however, it is not as explosive. Put your hand before your mouth and pronounce the words "pop" and "pipe". Your hand should feel a puff of air coming out of your mouth. Now pronounce the following Sicilian words: *pani, petra, pumu, papà* (bread, stone, apple, daddy). You should not have felt any air come out of your mouth, or at least not as much. Differentiate between the English and Sicilian "p" in pain/*pena*, poor/*pouru*, pidgeon/*picciuni*.

R

The **R** is trilled. It's pronounced by pointing the tip of the tongue toward the top of the upper front teeth. It can occur in medial position as in *soru, cori, amaru, scuru* (sister, heart, bitter, dark) and it's pronounced with a single trill. When double, the trill is stronger as it is in *carru, merru, ferru, guerra* (cart, blackbird, iron, war).

When it occurs in initial position, it is often doubled as in *rridiri, rragghiari, rraggiu, Rroma* (to laugh, to heehaw, ray, Rome). When the "r" is followed by another consonant in most parts of Sicily the "r" disappears and the following consonant is doubled, as in the following: *curpa/cuppa; mortu/mottu; corda/codda; porta/potta; curnutu/cunnutu* (fault, dead, cord, door, cuckold). In the area around Palermo, the same words will add a trailing "i" before the stressed vowel. Thus you will have *moittu, coidda, poitta, cuinnutu*.

S

S in Sicilian is like the English "s." In initial position and in medial position, it maintains the sound of the "s" as in Sam. Thus *sira, sali, sugnu, servu,* (salt, I am, servant) and *casa, spisa, stissu, vossia* (house, shopping, same, you) are all like the "s" in Sam. For double "s", apply the same rules as any double consonant, that is, pronounce the preceding vowel shorter. The "s" is pronounced like a "z" when it precedes a voiced consonant as in *sbulazzari* (to flutter), *sdintatu* (toothless) or *sminuzzari* (to break into small pieces) where the "b", "d" and the "m" are all voiced consonants. Preceding voiceless consonants, the "s" will be like the "s" of *sight* as in *scappari, scippari, scola, spagu, stubbitu, stazioni* (to flee, to pull out, school, thread, stupid, station).

A group of words written with an "s" present the peculiarity of changing the "s" sound into the "sci" sound in the eastern part of Sicily, around Messina. The sound is like the "ciu" of *ciuri*. Compare *cammisa, bbasari, cirasa, fasola, cusiri* (shirt, kiss, cherry, bean, to sew) with *cammicia, bbaciari, faciola, cuciri*.

We ought to point out that when the "s" is combined with the phoneme *tr* or *dr* the result is akin to the English pronunciation of "shrill" "shroud". Recall the peculiar sound of *trenu, drittu* (train, straight). Adding an "s" will cause a whistling sound between the teeth. Pronounce the following words: *strittu, strata, finestra, mastru, strummulu, seggiasdraia* and *strammu* (tight, street, window, master, spinning top, rocking chair and strange). Here Sicilian differs markedly from Italian.

In the province of Palermo and Trapani, the s before a voiceless consonant such as the p or t will be pronounced as in the English "shush". The following words *spisa, spata, stidda* will be pronounced "shpisa, shpata, shtidda."

T

The **T** is not the same as the English "t." It is not aspirated. The pronunciation of the expression *tutti i frutti,* which in American English sounds like **tudifrudi,** and *spaghetti,* which sounds more like *spaghedi,* clearly illustrates the difference. The "t" in Sicilian is formed by striking the upper front teeth with the tongue. Pronounce the following: *Tanu, timuri, stadda, stima, poti, potti, pattu, matina, muturi, carrettu.*

V

The **V** is primarily the same as the English "v" of *valiant.* Pronounce the following: *vinu, vinnigna, vita, vistina, vutti.* The "v" sometimes takes the place of the "b" in certain areas. Words such as *vutti, vucca, viviri, vinni* sometimes can be written and pronounced as *butti, bucca, biviri, binni.* Such dualities can give rise to misunderstandings as in the following dialogue between a judge and a defendant:

Judge—*To patri vivi?* Judge—Is your father alive?/ Does your father drink?

Defendant—*No, me patri litrìa.* —No, my father puts it away by liters.

Z

The **Z** is either equivalent to "tz" or "dz". In such words as *zeru, zabbara, zocculu,* it is a voiced consonant (dz) while in words like *zzappagghiuni, mazzu, azzioni, pazzu* it is a voiceless consonant (tz).

Phono-Syntactical Changes

When you pronounce words in a sentence each word has some effect on the words that follow. In this section we will examine some of the most important elements that can affect pronunciation.

The use of certain words results in the doubling of the initial consonant of the word that follows. Here are the most common words that cause the doubling:

The preposition *a.* "A Roma" (To Rome). Although "Roma" is written with a single "r", the combination will be pronounced "aRRoma". Similarly "a mia" (to me) *ammia,* "a tia" (to you) *attia,* and "a vui" (to you) would be written with a single consonant but pronounced double;

The verb *à* (has). In the phrase *Tu à ccapiri na cosa.* (You have to understand something) the "c" of "capiri" is pronounced double;

The words *ccà* and *ddà* (here, there). When combined with adverbs of place such as *sutta, fora, dintra,* (below, inside, outside) they become *ccassùtta, ddassùtta, ccaffòra, ddaffòra, ccaddìntra, ddad-dìntra* (down here, down there...);

The interrogative *chi* (what). Questions such as "what are you doing, what are you saying, what did you see?" will be pronounced *Chiffai? Chiddici? Chivvidisti?* The same thing happens also in exclamations preceded by "chi" as in *Chi vvirgogna! (What a shame!) Chi ttistazza!* (What a head!)

The verb *è* (is) and the conjunction *e* (and). In such combination as *è ggranni, è bberu, è bbonu, io e ttu* (it's big, it's true, it's good, I and you);

The 3rd person of the present of the verbs *fari, stari, putiri,* and **jiri**; as in, *fa mmali, sta vvicinu, pò ttrasiri, va ffora* (it hurts, lives close by, may come in, goes out);

The third person of the past tense of *essiri, fu* (was) as in the expression *fu cchissa a rraggiuni* (that was the reason).

The preposition *pri, (pi)* (for)as in *pri mmia, pri mme matri* (for me, for my mother);

Other monosyllables such as *tri, sì, su, sta, nè*;

Doubling can occur also with two-syllable words such as *quacchi, ogni* (some, every) as in *quacchivvota, ogniffimmina* (some time, every woman); even accented two-syllable words can cause doubling such as *pirchì, "pirchì vvinisti?"* (Why did you come?).

Diphthongs

Although the diphthongs will present no difficulty in terms of their pronunciation, we recognize that because they can take place in so many different ways they offer additional obstacles to understanding. Students need to be aware that in some areas of Sicily words having stressed *e* and *o* can often give way to the formation of diphthongs, that is two vowels instead of the one they replace, pronounced as one sound. For example words such as *ferru* (iron) may be pronounced as *fierru; pettu* (chest) as *piettu; ventu* (wind) as *vientu*, while *corvu* (crow) may be pronounced as *cuorvu*. In some *parrati* this may become *cuarvu; porcu, puorcu* or *puarcu*. The diphthongs in some areas are reduced to a single sound that is something in between, for example *felu* for *filu* or *molu* for *mulu* where the *e*

19

and the *o* have a mixed sound.

Such diphthongs regularly occur also in verbs affecting all persons except the first and second plural of the present tense. For example, the verb *circari* (to look for) and the verb *truvari* (to find) are normally conjugated as follows: *cercu, cerchi, cerca, circamu, circati, cercanu.* But in some areas where diphthongs occur it will conjugated as: *ciercu, cierchi, cerca, circamu, circati, cercanu*, while the verb *truvari* will have the normal conjugation as *trovu, trovi, trova, truvamu, truvati trovanu.* Where diphthongs occur, it will be *truovu, truovi, trova, truvamu, truvati, trovanu.*

Accents

Like Italian, Sicilian words are generally stressed on the next to the last syllable. *Amùri, piccirìddu, armàli, cùrtu* (love, little boy, animal, short). When the stress falls on the last syllable, the accent is written. Sicilian uses only the grave accent. Thus *pirchì, pò, ddà, ccà* (why, can, there, here). In Sicilian, the accent is used also where the corresponding Italian word has a different stress. In Italian the verb "persuad*è*re" (to persuade) has a stress on the next to the last *e*, where Sicilian "pirsuàdiri" the stress falls on the *a*. The third person plural endings of the imperfect are written with an accent: *avìanu, avèvanu, facìanu, liggìanu, jucàvanu, currèvanu.* This practice, however, is not uniform. Accents should be used to help the reader pronounce correctly. Sicilian also uses the circumflex accent to indicate that a contraction has taken place, that is, two elements have been fused together. Thus instead of writing "di lu" (of the) you may see *dû*; instead of "nta la" (in the) you may see *ntâ*, instead of "a lu" you may see *ô*.

There are other marks that affect the correct reading of texts such as the apostrophe and the aphaeresis. The apostrophe simply joins two words together by eliminating the vowel at the end of the first word as in *lu armali* (the animal) which becomes *l'armali, na acula* (an eagle) which becomes *n'acula*. The aphaeresis is also an apostrophe that indicates that an element has been left out of the word. The negative "nun" (not) drops the initial "n" and is replaced by an apostrophe. The same can be said of the preposition *in* where the "i" is replaced by the apostrophe. Sometimes words that were originally written *invidia, invitari,* and *invernu* in time lost the initial "i" and to indicate this many will write them with an apostrophe as follows *'nvidia, 'nvitari, 'nvernu.*

Intonation

The intonation of a sentence, in Italian or English, is an important element that adds significance to the statement. In Sicilian the intonation generally follows an undulating movement. Listen to the following sentence: *A signura Maria ìu a chesa stamatina.* (Maria went to church this morning) Notice how the voice rises and falls. Here is another utterance: *Me patri mi purtau a fera l'autru jornu.* (My father brought me to the fair the other day). When we are asking a question, however, the voice will rise at the end of the utterance. Here is an affirmative statement: *U prufissuri ci spiegau a lezzioni ê so studenti.* (The professor explained the lesson to his students). The same statement can become a question simply by changing the tone of the voice on pronouncing "ê so studenti?" : *U prufissuri ci spiegau a lezzioni ê so studenti?* Here is a statement followed by an exclamation mark: *Mizzica, quantu costa stu libru!* (Damn, this book is really expensive!) The voice will rise on pronouncing the first "i" of "mizzica" and dip when pronouncing the "o" of "costa". The same sentence read as a question: *Mizzica, quantu costa stu libru?* (Damn! How much does this book cost?) will pronounce "mizzica" as before but the the rest will dip toward the end. Generally If a question word such as "pirchì, "unni" "quannu" precedes the question the intonation will curve downward. *Pirchì vinisti?* (Why did you come?) If no question word is present the intonation will rise toward the end. *E' bedda Maria?* (Is Mary beautiful?) Although it's possible to change statements into questions by altering the intonation, often Sicilians will place the verb at the end of the question. Thus the following statement, *A signura Cuncetta havi a frevi.* (Cuncetta has a fever), can become a question by placing the verb at the end and changing the intonation upaward: *A signura Cuncetta a frevi havi?* or leaving the sentence as is and simply altering the intonation upwardly, *A signura Cuncetta havi a frevi?*

Appendices

Exercise 1: You will now hear ten words. Listen carefully and identify the word you hear spoken by underlining them in your text. The words will not be spoken in the same order as listed:

1. Matina 2. Signuruzzu 3. Grossu 4. Agneddu 5. Scannatu 6. Duminica 7. Spinsiratu 8. Vacabunnu 9. Munnizzaru 10. Cuteddu.

Exercise 2: Listen and repeat the following words:

1. Scimunitu 2. Scacciata 3.Mennuli 4. Buttigghia 5. Cacocciula 6. Vermi 7. Occhiu 8. Apparecchiu 9. Vriogna 10 Cazzottu

Exercise 3: The following words present special problems discussed in the preceding pages. They represent contrastive pairs which highlight the difference between double and single consonants. Your task is to identify which word contains double consonants, the first or the second one. Check your answers on page 26.

	first	*second*
1.	____	____
2.	____	____
3	____	____
4	____	____
5	____	____
6	____	____
7	____	____
8	____	____
9	____	____
10	____	____

Exercise 4: You will hear ten words. Mark the syllable that is stressed by putting an accent on it. Check your answers on p. 27.

1. Amichevuli 2. Annivirsariu 3. Picciutteddu 4. Pecura 5. Picuruni 6. Persicu 7. Mamciavanu 8. Avianu 9. Ficazzana 10. Voluntati.

Exercise 5: This is a more difficult exercise. Try to identify where doubling occurred by writing the additional consonant where you heard it. Check your answers on page 27.

1. Pri mia, va beni. 2. Pirchì vinisti ora? 3. Fa pena a vidirlu. 4. Chi dissi;' 5. E poi chi fici? 6. E tu non veni? 7. Chi razza di cristianu è? 8. Comu fu fu! 9. Si veru tintu! 10. Accussì caru e?

Exercise 6: You will hear ten words containing the difficult sound we have been writing with "ciu". Listen and repeat the words:

1. Ciumara 2. ciuri 3. Ciurera 4. ciusciari 5. ciatu 6. ciauni 7. ciocca 8. ciauru 9. Ciariati 10. ciamma.

Exercise 7: You will hear words some of which contain a double "d" or the retroflex "dd" sound. Identify the words with retroflex sounds by underlining them. Check your answers on page 27.

1. s'addurmisciu 2. s'addunau 3. s'addinucchiau 4. madduni 5.Biddazzu 6. addumanna 7. cuteddu 8. fuddittu 9. addiventa 10. muddica.

Exercise 8: You will hear a little dialogue between a store owner and a client. From *Arba Sicula* XXII, 2004. The *parrata* is from the Aeolian Islands. Follow the dialogue and repeat it until you have the intonation right.

Scena Tra Putiaru e Clienti
di Amedeo Re

Clienti : Rosa; Putiaru : Don Cicciu

Rosa: Bon giornu, Don Cicciu! Cuantu costa un paru di mutanni?

Don Cicciu: Milli e triccentu liri, Rosuzza.

Rosa: E sta cammisa riccamata quant'è?

Don Cicciu: Ottucentu liri, ciatuzzu miu!

Rosa: Vih, finimula cu stu scherzu! I priezzi sunnu auti e vossia m'avi a fari nu scuntu.

Don Cicciu: Siccomu mi fai geniu, Rosa mia, facimu accussì: i mutanni milli e cientu liri e a cammisa milli liri, picchì sì tu!

Rosa: Va, va, Don Cicciu! Chi modu esti chissu di trattari i cristiani? Vossia mi isa a cammisa e mi cala i mutanni!

Scene is Clothing Store
by Amedeo Re

Customer: Rosa; Owner: Don Cicciu

Rosa: Good morning, Don Cicciu! How much is this pair of panties?

Don Cicciu: One thousand three hundred lire, my dear Rosy.

Rosa: And this embroidered blouse, how much?

Don Cicciu: Eight hundred lire, my sweet Rosy.

Rosa: Go on, Let's stop this game. The prices are too high. You have to give me a discount.

Don Cicciu: Because I like you so much, Rosy, I will offer you a deal: the panties a thousand one hundred and the blouse a thousand, but just for vou!

Rosa: Go on, Don Cicciu! What way of treating customers is this? You're raising my blouse and lowering my panties!

Exercise 9: The following is a famous poem by Ignazio Buttitta that expresses the chagrin of a people who are losing the language inherited from their ancestors. It is a poem written in defense of the Sicilian language. Listen to it twice. The second time, fill in the word that have been left out of the text below. Check your answers with the answers on p. 27.

Lingua e dialettu
Un populu mittitilu a catina

1_____

attuppaticci a vucca,
è ancora libiru
Livaticci u passaportu
a tavula unni 2 _____
u lettu unni dormi
è ancora riccu.
Un populu,
diventa poviru e servu
quannu ci arrobbanu a lingua
addutata di patri:

e persu 3 _____
Diventa poviru e servu,
quannu i paroli
nun 4_____ paroli
e si mancianu tra d'iddi
Mi nn'addugnu ora,
mentri accordu a 5 _____
dti dialettu
ca perdi na corda lu jornu.
Mentri arripezzu
   6 _____camuluta
chi tisseru i nostri avi
cu lana di pecuri siciliani.

   E sugnu 7 _____
haiu i dinari
e non li pozzu spenniri
i giuelli
e non li pozzu rigalari;
u cantu,
nta gaggia
   cu l'ali 8 _____
Un poviru,
c'addatta ntê minni strippi
da matri putativa,
chi u chiama figghiu
pi 9 _____
Nuatri l'avevamu a matri,
nni l'arrubbaru;
aveva i minni a funtana di latti
e ci vippiru tutti,
   ora ci 10 _____
Nni ristò a vuci d'idda,
a cadenza
a nota vascia
dû sonu e dû lamentu
Chissi non nni ponnu

rubbari,
Nni ristò a sumigghianza,
l'annatura,
i gesti,
i lampi nta l'occhi:
chissi non nni ponnu rubbari
Non 'ni ponnu rubbari,
ma ristamu poviri,
e orfani u stissu,

Language and Dialect

Put a people in chains,
strip them naked,
plug up their mouths,
they are still free;
take away their passports
the place where they eat,
the bed where they sleep,
they are still rich.
A people become
poor and enslaved
when you rob them of their tongue
handed down by their forefathers:
they are lost forever.
They become poor and enslaved
when their words
don't father other words
and they devour one another.
I realize it now,
as I tune my dialect guitar
that is losing
a string every day.
As I patch up
the worm-eaten tapestry
our ancestors wove
with wool of Sicilian sheep.

And I am poor,
I have money
but I cannot spend it;
I have jewels
and I can't give them away;
the song inside a cage,
with its wings chopped off.
Like a poor man sucking
at the withered teat
of a putative mother
who calls him son
as a way of mocking him.
We had a mother once,
She was stolen from us;
her breasts were fountains of milk
and all once drank from them,
now they spit on them.
Her voice has remained,
her cadence,
that deep low note
of the sound and lament.
No one can steal these from us.
We bear her resemblance,
the way she walked,
her gestures,
the lightning flashes in our eyes.
No one can steal these from us.
No one can steal them,
but we remain poor,
and orphans, just the same.

Li Cosi di Diu"
Di Berto Giambalvo
(Storii in parrata tra[aanisa, edituri)

Avia quasi trentacinc'anni, la facci comu un squarateddu, riccu assa di saluti ma scarsu, p'un diri orvu, di sapiri. Un-gnornu pinza: "Ora mi maritu e mmi cuetu". Sciu tutti li carti chi cci vosiru e li purtà a lu parrinu p'appizzari li bbanni a lu parabentu. Lu paracu cci detti na taliata, fici finta chi si pirsuariu, poi cci dissi:

-- Tu avissi a-bbeniri na quinnicina di iorna ccà, ala duttrina, pi zignariti li cosi di Ddiu e –ppi sapiri comu si fa nta la vita maritata.

Lu Bbatassanu lu talia e-ddopu um-pezzu rrispunniu:

-- Patri paracu, ie chi-ppozzu perdiri ssu tempu: 'aiu un-zaccu di chiffari!

Ci pari chi sugnu sfacinnatu? Eppoi, a-ttrentacinc'anni, ch'aiu bbisognu di sapillu di vossia chi si fa nta la vita maritata?

Lu paracu -- unn affinnennu l'abbitu -- avia na crozza chi si nni futtia di Bbatassanu. Era vecchiu ottrantinu - Si chiamava patri Sarvaggiu - cu na tonaca ngrasciata, nzunzata di fetu di Cira e dd' ncenzu chi lassava na maniata chi un cristianu cu lu cimurru la sintia, e aisannu la vuci ci dissi chi lu matrimoniu è un-zacramentu e unn è cchiddu chi ppenzi tu, e si nun zai li cosi di Ddiu, 'un ti maritu, Bbatassanu nni vulia fari una di li so, ma era nta 1a chiesa e si trattinni. Si nni va senza mancu salutallu, ma pinzava chi s'avia a maritari e un-zapia a ccu diri di metticci 1a bbona parola. Penza a-mmia e mi veni a trova:-Salutamu.

-- Salutamu.

-- Frate, tu cci nn'a amicizzia cu lu paracu di san Giuvanni?

-- Picchì, chi ti successi;-

-- Stu disgrazziatu 'un mi voli maritari picchì dici ch'à sapiri pi forza li cosi di Diu, cu cci ha cummattutu mai? Mi nn'av'a fari fuiri? Chi aiu quinnici anni? 'Viri si cci po' parlari, tra vuiatri vi capiti.

-- Ti pari ch'è ffacili pirsuariri ssa crozza? Dumani a la lintata manu nni viremu davanti a la chiesa...

"The Things of God"
by Berto Giambalvo,
Translated into English by Gaetano Cipolla.

He was almost thirty-five years old with a face like burned round bread, very rich in health but rather poor, if not totally devoid, of knowledge. One day he thought "Now I will get married and this way I settle down." He asked for all the documents he needed and brought them to the parish priest so he could post the wedding bands. The priest looked them over, made believe he was in agreement, then he said to him: "You ought to spend at least two weeks here, in order to become acquainted with Catechism and to learn how to behave when you are married."

Baldassarre looked at him and after a while he replied: "Father, how can I spend two weeks with you. I have a load of things to do. You think I am unemployed? And besides, at thirty-five years of age, do you think I need to learn from you what one does when one is married?"

The priest, without offense to his vestments, had a head that could not care less for Baldassarre's words. He was old, in his eighties—his name was Father Sarvaggiu—and wore a tunic so dirty with the stench of wax and incense that if you had a double cold you still could smell it. Father Sarvaggiu raised his voice and told him that matrimony is a sacrament and "it's not what you are thinking of... and if you don't learn Catechism I won't marry you!" Baldassarre felt like replying in tone but since he was in church he held back and went away without saying goodbye. But he was determined to get married and pondered who might be able to put in a good word for him. He thought of me and came to see me.

-Greetings.

-Greetings.

-Brother, are you in good terms with the priest of St. Giovanni's Church?

-Why, what happened to you?

-That uncouth priest does not want to marry me because he says I need to learn Catechism. Who's ever heard of that? Does he want me to run away with her? What am I, fifteen years old? See if you can speak to him: the two of you understand each other.

-You think it's easy to persuade a head like his? Let's meet tomorrow after work in front of the church...

Exercise 11. Listen to the following poem by Nino Martoglio in the *parrata* of Catania. From *The Poetry of Nino Martoglio*. NY: Legas, 1993.

Nica

Nica, tu fusti babba: mi lassasti
cridennu ca ju tuttu t'avia datu,
e tuttu chiddu chi tegnu sarvatu
ancora non è to', e ci l'appizzasti...
Quantu carizzi chi non hai pruvatu!
Quantu piaciri chini di cuntrasti!
Babba chi sì, pirchì m'abbannunasti,
si lu me saccu 'un'era sbacantatu?

Ju sacciu dari certi vasuneddi
supra lu coddu, accostu a li capiddi,
chi fannu li carnuzzi stiddi stiddi...
Sacciu 'ncantari sulu ca m'affacciu
dintra l'ucchiuzzi di li beddi...Sacciu...
Ma, Nica! A cu talii, cu ss'occhi friddi?

Nica

Nica, what foolish thing you've done! You left me,
thinking I'd given you all I possessed.
But everything I kept inside my heart
was not yet yours: and now you've lost that part!
So many sweet caresses you've not had!
So many varied and contrasting pleasures!
Ah, foolish girl! What did you leave me for
when in my sack there was still so much more?

I know how to give kisses, oh so light,
around the neck, a bit below the hairline,
that make girls' flesh all tingly with delight...
I know how to enchant with one brief gaze
into the eyes of fair young maids...I know...
But, Nica, why such coldness in your eyes?

Answers to the Exercises

Exercise 3: Contrastive pairs of single and double consonants:
1. Caru- carru
2. Vini-vinni
3. Nanna- nana
4. Spisa- spissu
5. Jattu-jatu
6. Cottu-cotu
7. Assai- usai
8. Potti-poti
9. Viti- vitti
10. Ccani-cani

Exercise 4: The stress is indicated by the letter in italics.
1. Amich*e*vuli 2 . Annivirs*a*riu 3. Picciutt*e*ddu 4. P*e*cura 5. Picur*u*ni 6. P*e*rsicu 7. Manci*a*vanu 8. Av*i*anu 9. Ficazz*a*na 10.Volunt*a*ti

Exercise 5: The bold consonants resulted from the doubling.
1. Pri **mm***ia va bbeni.*
2. Pirchì **vv***inisti ora,*
3. Fa **pp***ena a* **vv***idirlu.*
4. Chi **dd***issi?*
5. E **pp***oi chi ffici?*
6. E **tt***u non veni?*
7. Chi **rr***azza di cristianu è?*
8. Comu fu **ff***u!*
9. Sì **vv***eru tintu!*

10. Accussì **ccaru** *è?*

Exercise 7: The retroflex sounds are indicated by the Italics.
1. s'addurmiscìu
2. s'addunau
3. s'addinucchiau
4. ma*ddu*ni
5. Bi*dda*zzu
6. addumanna
7. Cute*ddu*
8. fiu*ddi*ttu
9. addiventa
10. Mu*ddi*ca.

Exercise 9. These words were left out of the poem "Lingua e dialettu."
   1. spugghiatilu
   2. mancia
   3. pi sempri
   4. figghianu
   5. chitarra
   6. a tila
   7. poviru
   8. tagghiati
   9. pi 'nciuria
   10. sputanu.